EXTREME

Pets Parents Hate!

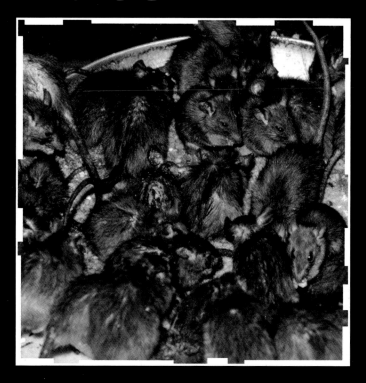

Trevor Day

A & C Black • London

Produced for A & C Black by

MONKEY PUZZLE MEDIA LTD — Monkey Puzzle Media Ltd
The Rectory, Eyke, Woodbridge
Suffolk IP12 2QW, UK

Published by A & C Black Publishers Limited
38 Soho Square, London W1D 3HB

First published 2008
Copyright © 2008 A & C Black Publishers Limited

ISBN 978-1-4081-0013-4 (hardback)
ISBN 978-1-4081-0098-1 (paperback)

The right of Trevor Day to be identified as the
author of this Work has been asserted by him in
accordance with the Copyright, Designs and Patents
Act 1988.

A CIP catalogue record for this book is available
from the British Library.

Editor: Cath Senker
Design: Mayer Media Ltd
Picture research: Lynda Lines
Series consultant: Jane Turner

This book is produced using paper that is made
from wood grown in managed, sustainable forests.
It is natural, renewable and recyclable. The logging
and manufacturing processes conform to the
environmental regulations of the country of origin.

Printed in China by C & C Offset Printing Co., Ltd

Picture acknowledgements
Alamy p. 25 top (Arco Images); Corbis pp. 1 (Jeffrey
L Rotman), 10 (Tom Brakefield), 15 (Tim Davis), 24
(Jeffrey L Rotman); FLPA pp. 7 (Mark Moffett/
Minden Pictures), 11 (Mark Moffett/Minden Pictures),
13 (Nigel Cattlin), 19 (Chris Mattison), 23 (Angela
Hampton), 25 bottom (Michael Krabs/Imagebroker),
29 (RP Lawrence); Getty Images pp. 8–9 (Frank
Greenaway), 28 (AFP); iStockphoto pp. 5 (Holly
Kuchera), 6, 14 (Feng Yu); NHPA p. 20 (Anthony
Bannister); Photographers Direct p. 16 (Helena
Kadlcikova); Photolibrary.com pp. 12, 17
(E Degginger), 18 (Vivek Sinha); Rex Features p. 27
(Geoff Moore); RSPCA Photolibrary p. 22 (Angela
Hampton); Science Photo Library pp. 4 (David
Aubrey), 21 top (MH Sharp), 26 (Alan Carey); Still
Pictures p. 21 bottom (Biosphoto/Gunther Michel).

The front cover shows a Mexican red-knee
tarantula (Getty Images/Brian Stablyk).

CONTENTS

Disclaimer
None of these pets should be kept without adult supervision. As will become clear, some of these animals should not be kept as pets at all.

Abbreviations **m** stands for metres • **ft** stands for feet • **in** stands for inches • **cm** stands for centimetres • **g** stands for grams • **lb** stands for pounds

Pets parents hate

Several million types of animal live on the planet. They range from tiny ants to whales as big as aircraft. A few thousand kinds are kept as pets. Some make better housemates than others.

Venomous (poisonous) sting used to kill **prey** and to defend itself

Parents will probably hate dangerous pets, such as scorpions. Most will certainly dislike smelly skunks. Even cute pets take up space. They all need food, water and a safe, comfortable place to live.

The maps in this book show where each animal comes from.

Some people keep imperial scorpions, like this one, as pets.

Claws for grabbing prey

prey a creature that is eaten by other creatures

Pet skunks are active and love to play. They need plenty of attention. When scared, a skunk arches its back and lifts its tail to make itself look bigger. If it is very frightened, it squirts stinky **fluid** from two nozzles near its tail.

The black bear cub has frightened the skunk. The cub may get a smelly surprise!

Stinking skunks

The scientific name for a skunk is *Mephitis mephitis*, meaning "stinks, stinks".

fluid a liquid – a runny substance

Praying mantis — the Kung Fu fighter

What has an insect got to do with humans fighting? One style of Kung Fu is based on the moves of the praying mantis.

The praying mantis gets its name because its front legs look like they are being held out in prayer. The insect strikes its prey by whipping its front legs forward. It stabs the victim's weakest parts. Then the praying mantis eats its victim alive. The insect's moves inspired Wang Lang, one of the people who created Kung Fu.

Pet praying mantises should be kept alone in a tank. Otherwise they will attack each other.

Live prey

A pet praying mantis needs live insects, such as flies or grasshoppers, to eat. You can buy them from a pet shop – or catch them yourself.

A praying mantis should be kept among plants so that it can hide.

6

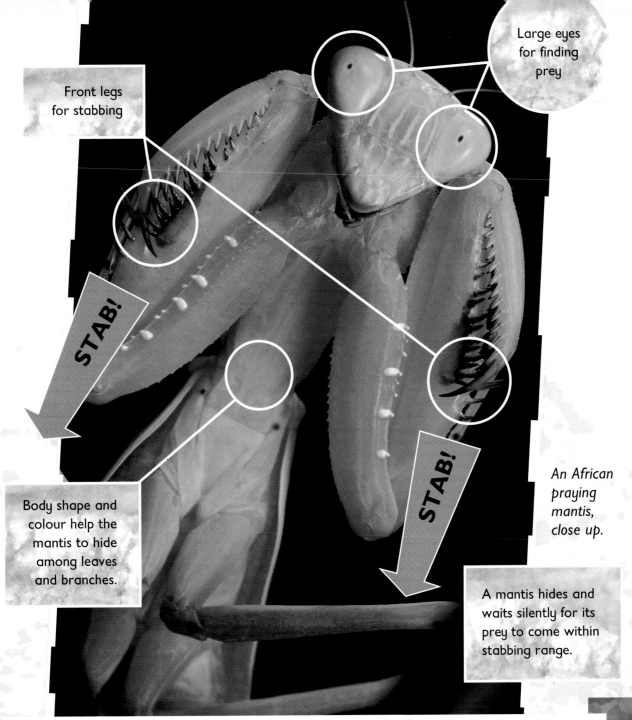

Large eyes for finding prey

Front legs for stabbing

STAB!

Body shape and colour help the mantis to hide among leaves and branches.

STAB!

An African praying mantis, close up.

A mantis hides and waits silently for its prey to come within stabbing range.

insect a six-legged animal with a hard outer skeleton and a body divided into three parts

How many legs?
Millipedes and centipedes

Millipedes and centipedes both have many legs. The biggest animals grow to about 25 centimetres (10 inches) long. One of them bites. The other does not. Which is which?

Peruvian giant orange leg centipede.

A lot of legs

Millipedes (from the Latin for "thousand legs") in fact have between 100 and 700 legs. Centipedes ("hundred legs") have between 30 and 160.

Hard, glossy outer skeleton gives protection

Large body segments

One pair of legs for each **segment**

segment a repeated main part of the body

Antennae for sensing smells and vibrations in the dark

Before you decide to have a pet, you should find out about the animal. Millipedes make good pets. They feed on bits of dead plants and animals. When frightened, they curl up.

Big centipedes are not such good pets. They are predators – they hunt other animals. Centipedes inject **venom** into their prey with their fangs to overpower it. They could bite you too!

Ouch!
Fangs inject venom

Joints between each segment allow the body to bend.

venom poison

Hairy housemates: tarantulas

Imagine your mum or dad opening the curtains to find a large, hairy tarantula staring them in the face. Is your poor parent in danger?

In fact, tarantulas can make great pets, if you choose the right type and treat them carefully. If a tarantula bites you, it is usually no worse than a wasp sting.

Some types of tarantula live on the ground, while others prefer trees. Some are **solitary**, but others live in groups. Check so you can give the tarantula the right surroundings and food. It will eat crickets, mealworms, large flies, or even small dead mice.

Sting shocks

A few people are **allergic** to tarantula bites. They may go into shock and even stop breathing. An injection of a drug called adrenaline stops the shock.

The Chilean rose tarantula is a solitary, ground-living spider. Tarantulas can grow to the size of a man's hand.

---

allergic become ill when the body reacts badly to a particular substance   **solitary** living alone

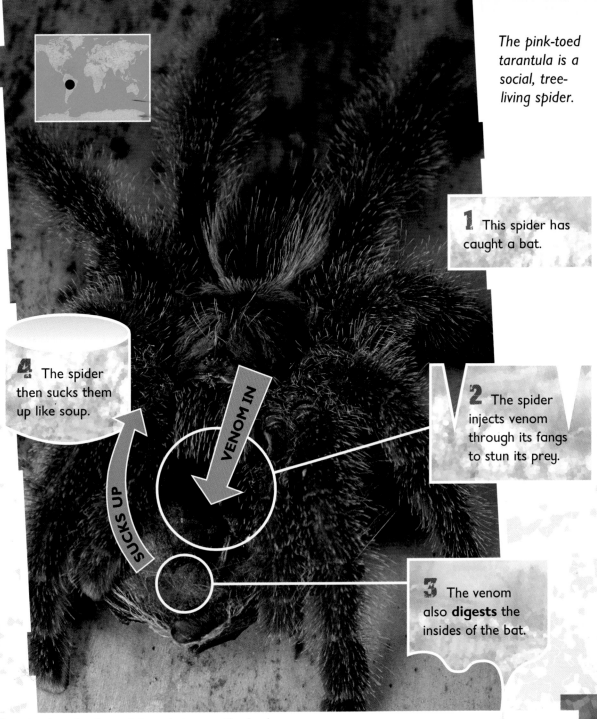

The pink-toed tarantula is a social, tree-living spider.

1 This spider has caught a bat.

2 The spider injects venom through its fangs to stun its prey.

3 The venom also **digests** the insides of the bat.

4 The spider then sucks them up like soup.

VENOM IN

SUCKS UP

digests breaks down into substances the body can use

On the trail of a snail

You'll know where a pet snail has been from the glistening slimy trail that it leaves behind. This will not make your parents happy.

African land snails with their young.

Fast breeder

Every snail is both male and female. Any two adults can **fertilize** each other. They can each lay several hundred eggs in a year.

fertilize when a sperm joins with an egg to make a new individual

Some people love keeping African land snails as pets because they look so strange. Their body changes shape, they hide inside the shell, or they stretch out and slide around. These snails are not allowed into the United States of America in case they escape, breed and munch crops. They have a giant appetite for juicy leaves.

The giant African land snail can grow to more than 15 cm (6 in) long and weigh a massive 450 g (1 lb).

A snail needs to eat plenty of calcium to make its chalky shell. Egg shells or **cuttlebone** can provide this.

Uh-oh!
The snail hides in its spiral shell when threatened.

Slime!
Mucus trail

Scratchy!
Rough tongue shreds leafy food

Tentacles (eyes on stalks)

cuttlebone skeleton of a cuttlefish   **mucus** slime made by animals

Piranhas: fancy a bite?

Piranha fish have teeth that cut like sharp scissors. Some people say that a shoal of piranha can strip a living horse or human to the bone in minutes. Is this the kind of fish you'd like to keep in your bedroom?

Don't keep your piranha with smaller fish. It will eat them!

Piranha are not really as scary as they seem. Even starving piranha rarely attack large animals. Very few horses and people have ever been killed in this way – but it has happened. Piranha usually live in South American rivers. They nip the scales and fins of larger fish and feed on dead animals. Piranha also eat plants.

You can keep a piranha as a pet in a tank of clean, warm, fresh (not salty) water at 24–28°C (75–83°F). Make sure it has places to hide. You should feed it fish food and sometimes offer fresh vegetables. Remember – don't waggle your fingers in the water!

Toothy devil

The name "piranha" comes from native languages in Brazil. It means "tooth fish" or "devil fish".

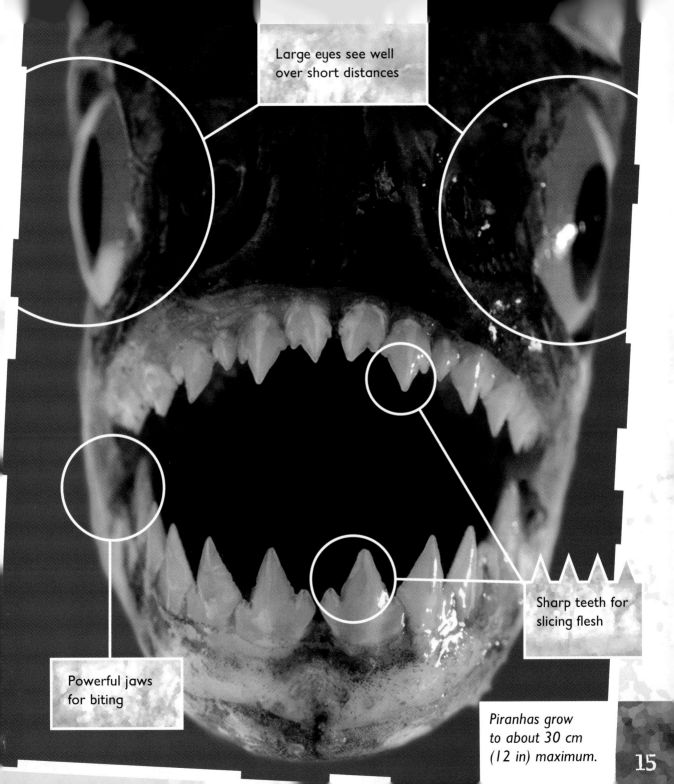

Large eyes see well over short distances

Sharp teeth for slicing flesh

Powerful jaws for biting

Piranhas grow to about 30 cm (12 in) maximum.

Slippery customers: frogs

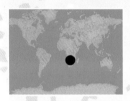

The water should be shallow so the frog can stand on the bottom and reach up to breathe air.

The creepy-looking African clawed frog is covered in protective slime. It's more slippery than a bar of soap. If it escapes, just try catching it!

Frogs and toads are **amphibians**. They live partly in water and partly on land. A pet African clawed frog needs a tank of clean, fresh water.

Jumpy

Frogs jump. One South African frog did a triple jump of about 10 metres (more than 33 feet)! Make sure the tank has a secure lid so a pet frog can't escape.

amphibian slimy animal with a backbone that lives both in water and on land

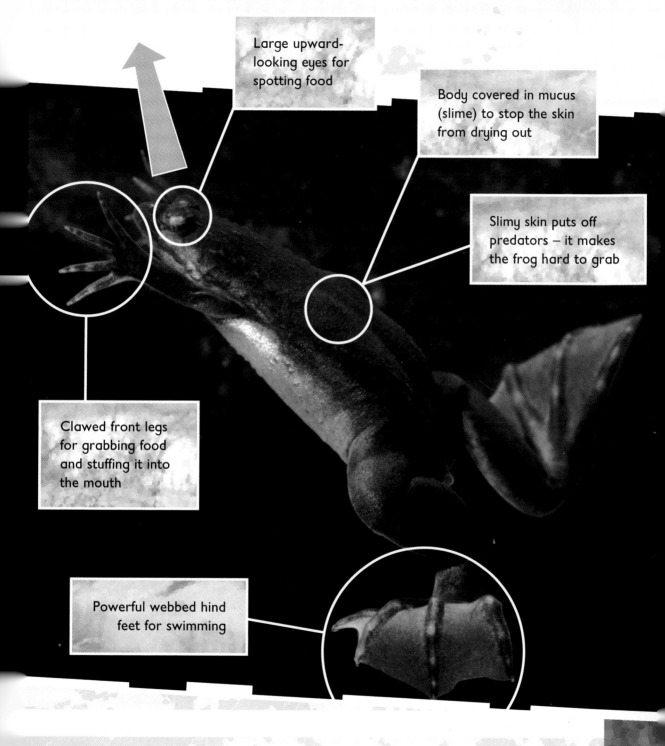

Large upward-looking eyes for spotting food

Body covered in mucus (slime) to stop the skin from drying out

Slimy skin puts off predators — it makes the frog hard to grab

Clawed front legs for grabbing food and stuffing it into the mouth

Powerful webbed hind feet for swimming

Quite a mouthful: pythons

Before you buy a pet snake, check how large it will become!

In Florida, USA, some people buy baby Burmese pythons as pets. Then they discover that the snakes grow to 2 metres (6 feet) long in one year. Some owners can't cope and they release them into the wild. The pythons grow even bigger – up to 5–7 metres (16–23 feet) long. They're big enough to swallow alligators!

Burmese python catching a rabbit.

How dangerous?

Out of about 3,000 kinds of snakes, only around one in ten are venomous (poisonous). Of these, fewer than 100 are dangerous to people.

suffocates dies from lack of air

The Burmese python coils around its prey, squeezing it tightly. The prey can no longer breathe. It **suffocates** and dies. The python swallows the animal head first. Its jaws and stomach stretch to make room for the enormous meal.

The royal python is a popular pet. For a python, it is small. Like other pythons, it is not venomous.

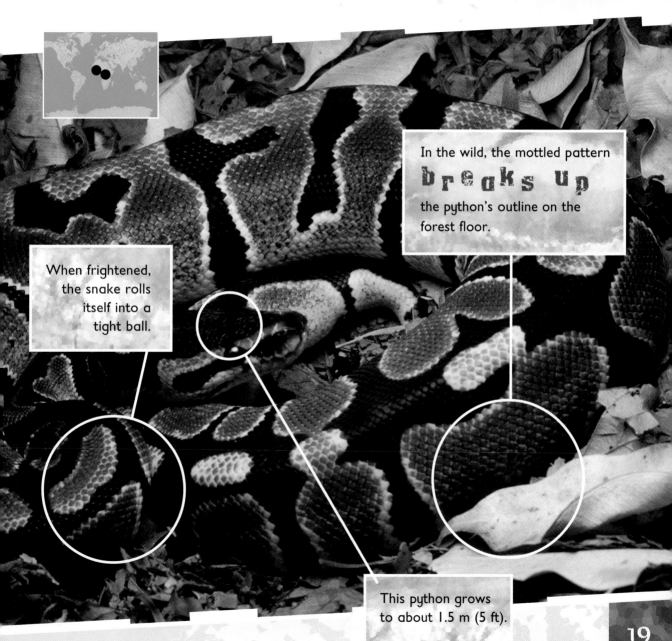

In the wild, the mottled pattern **breaks up** the python's outline on the forest floor.

When frightened, the snake rolls itself into a tight ball.

This python grows to about 1.5 m (5 ft).

Toothy smiles: crocs

How would you like to find a crocodile in your bath? Surprisingly, some people used to keep crocodiles and alligators. Their toothy bite made them dangerous pets.

A crocodile has a long snout. You can see the fourth lower tooth when its jaw is shut.

The Nile crocodile is a feared man-eater in many African countries. Crocodiles can float with only their eyes and nostrils showing above the water. This makes them hard to spot.

Going, going ...

Of 23 types of **crocodilian**, four are likely to die out within a few years, unless people take action to save them.

crocodilian a crocodile, alligator or caiman

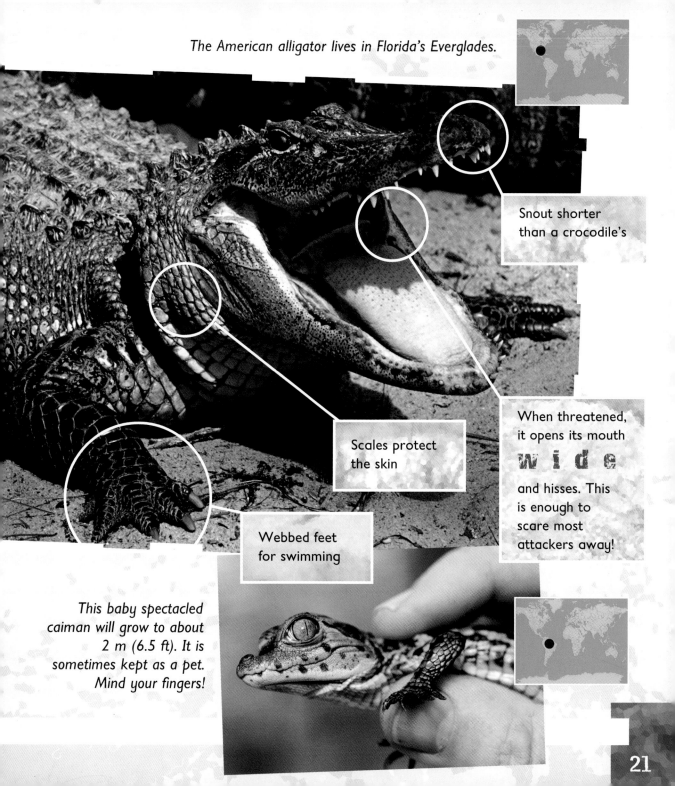

The American alligator lives in Florida's Everglades.

Snout shorter than a crocodile's

Scales protect the skin

When threatened, it opens its mouth **w i d e** and hisses. This is enough to scare most attackers away!

Webbed feet for swimming

This baby spectacled caiman will grow to about 2 m (6.5 ft). It is sometimes kept as a pet. Mind your fingers!

Not so bird brained!

Imagine your mum or dad has an important visitor round when a voice calls out, "Hey, ugly!" – or something much worse! You can blame it on the parrot.

Key, ugly!

Bird-brained means stupid, but some birds are far from stupid. A scientist in Arizona, USA taught her grey parrot Alex to recognize and ask for more than 50 different things.

Be careful what you teach your bird! It will copy your voice and

A grey parrot can live for 50 years. Parrots have their own characters, just like people do.

your words. Parrots like to mimic sounds – everything from doorbells, to telephone rings, to burps and farts, to barking dogs.

Deadly dangers

Some common things around the house or garden are deadly to parrots. Avocado pears and buttercup or rhubarb leaves are poisonous. Tobacco smoke is too.

The parrot tears off a piece of cooked bone with its bill.

Upper bill used for **hooking** branches or perch when climbing

Point of lower bill used for **cracking** seeds and nuts

Four toes for **grasping** its perch

Rats rule

With its sharp teeth, a rat on the loose can nibble your books, gnaw the TV wires and ruin your best furniture. This is a pet your parents may truly hate.

Wild rats bite and carry diseases. In Europe in the **Middle Ages**, fleas from black rats passed on a disease called bubonic **plague**. Between 1347 and 1351, the plague killed one third of European people. Wild rats also carry diseases in their urine and droppings.

For the priests at a temple in Deshnok, India, the rats are holy. The priests care for the rats and even share their feeding bowls. If a visitor accidentally hurts a rat, he or she must pay the priests in gold or silver.

Fast breeder!

A female rat can produce 6–12 babies every few weeks. If all her babies survive and breed, she will leave behind 1,000 rats in a year.

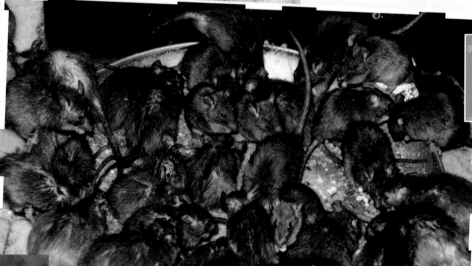

In the Deshnok temple, India, 20,000 rats run free.

Middle Ages the time between the 5th and 15th centuries

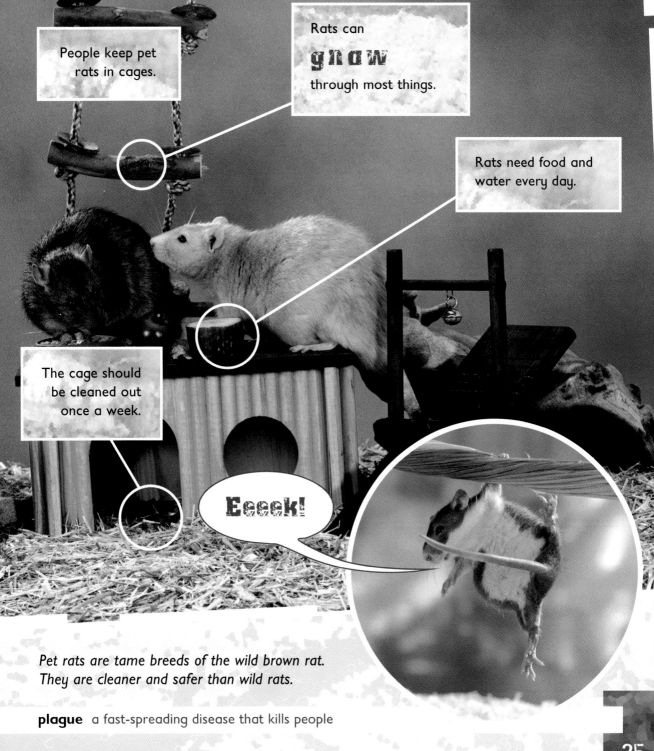

People keep pet rats in cages.

Rats can **gnaw** through most things.

Rats need food and water every day.

The cage should be cleaned out once a week.

Eeeek!

Pet rats are tame breeds of the wild brown rat. They are cleaner and safer than wild rats.

plague a fast-spreading disease that kills people

Ferreting around

Ferrets live life in the fast lane. In the wild, they are a blur of fur. Kept as pets, these sleek bundles of energy demand lots of attention.

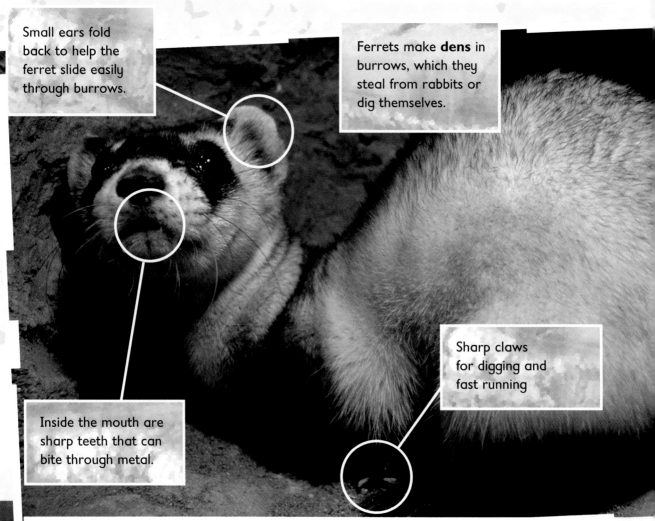

Small ears fold back to help the ferret slide easily through burrows.

Ferrets make **dens** in burrows, which they steal from rabbits or dig themselves.

Sharp claws for digging and fast running

Inside the mouth are sharp teeth that can bite through metal.

den shelter

Ferrets need exercise. Some owners race them against other ferrets.

A ferret is a tame European polecat, a type of weasel. In the wild, polecats chase rats, mice and rabbits. They even attack animals larger than themselves. After catching their prey, they give it a "kill bite" on the neck.

A pet ferret is quite a handful! It can be dangerous if not properly trained and should be kept in a strong cage. If a ferret escapes, it can attack other pets and even babies.

Hide and seek

Ferrets need to explore and play. They should be let out for two to three hours each day. Watch out! Ferrets will hunt down all kinds of things — such as socks and keys — and hide them.

Hogging the limelight

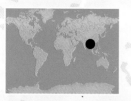

The actor George Clooney used to live with a pot-bellied pig called Max. The pig came on film shoots with George, and sometimes even slept in his bed!

A pot-bellied pig looks cute when young, but grows to become heavier than a man.

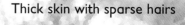
Thick skin with sparse hairs

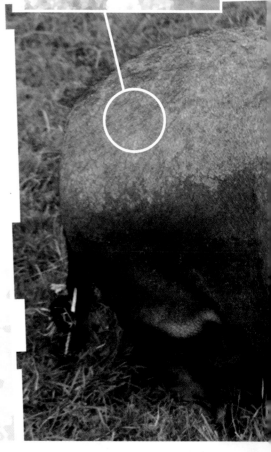

enclosure piece of land with a fence or wall around it

There was a craze for pot-bellied pigs in the 1960s and 1970s. Some were bought for thousands of pounds. Many were later given away to pig **sanctuaries** when they grew too big.

Max once went for a ride in actor John Travolta's plane: so pigs do, in fact, fly. Max, weighing in at about 135 kilograms (300 pounds), died in 2006 at the age of 18.

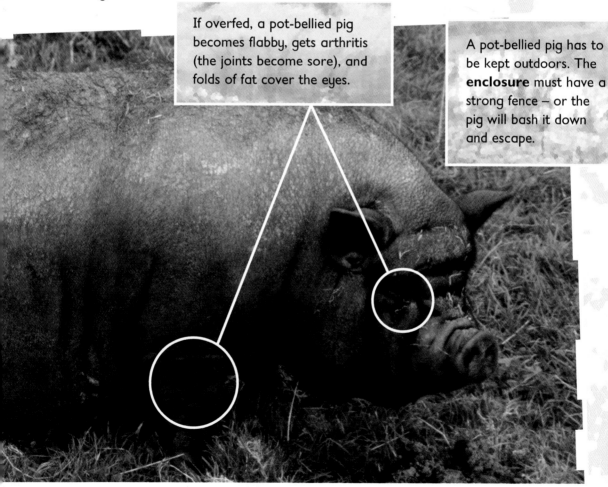

If overfed, a pot-bellied pig becomes flabby, gets arthritis (the joints become sore), and folds of fat cover the eyes.

A pot-bellied pig has to be kept outdoors. The **enclosure** must have a strong fence – or the pig will bash it down and escape.

sanctuary place where wild animals are protected

Glossary

allergic become ill when the body reacts badly to a particular substance

amphibian slimy animal with a backbone that lives both in water and on land

crocodilian a crocodile, alligator or caiman

cuttlebone skeleton of a cuttlefish

den shelter

digests breaks down into substances the body can use

enclosure piece of land with a fence or wall around it

fertilize when a sperm joins with an egg to make a new individual

fluid a liquid – a runny substance

insect a six-legged animal with a hard outer skeleton and a body divided into three parts

Middle Ages the time between the 5th and 15th centuries

mucus slime made by animals

plague a fast-spreading disease that kills people

prey a creature that is eaten by other creatures

sanctuary place where wild animals are protected

segment a repeated main part of the body

solitary living alone

suffocates dies from lack of air

venom poison

TOP TIPS FOR CHOOSING A PET

1. Have you checked the pet species (type) you want? Only then can you find out what you need to keep it. Ask for advice and read about your pet. Make sure you have everything ready before the pet arrives.

2. Are there any dangers in keeping the pet? The pet might bite, or someone might be allergic to it.

3. Check with other people in your home that they are happy to have this pet.

4. Are you prepared to look after the pet, not just now, but in one year or five years time? Who will look after it when you are on holiday?

5. Will a new pet get along with any other pets in your house?

6. Who will pay for looking after your pet – the food, equipment and vet's bills?

7. Is your pet legal? For example, it is illegal to keep ferrets in some states of the United States of America.

8. Buy your pet from someone you trust. Does the person have experience of keeping the animal?

9. Make sure you choose a pet that is healthy and strong.

If you and your family are happy with your answers to all the tips, then go for it!

Further information

Books

Exotic Pets (Collins Need to Know) by David Manning (Collins, 2008)
Tips for caring for unusual household pets, such as lizards, snakes, frogs, newts and creepy crawlies.

Snakes by Sonia Hernandez-Divers (Heinemann, 2003)
A young person's introduction to keeping these fascinating reptiles.

The Exotic Pet Handbook by David Alderton (Southwater, 2003)
A family-friendly guide to all kinds of unusual pets, including insects, fish, amphibians, reptiles and birds.

Youch! It Bites! by Trevor Day (Simon & Schuster, 2000)
Scary pictures and fascinating facts about animals that bite, stab or sting.

Great Pets! An Extraordinary Guide to Usual and Unusual Family Pets by Sara Stein (Storey Publishing, 2003)
A bumper guide to more than 60 types of pet. Includes what makes them interesting and how to look after each kind.

Keeping Creepy Crawlies by Dave Clark (Barron's Educational Series, Hauppauge, 2000)
Amazing facts and practical information on keeping invertebrates as pets.

Websites

http://exoticpets.about. com/
A window into the world of unusual pets.

www.aspca.org/site/ PageServer?pagename= kids_home
Animaland. Fun and good advice from the American Society for the Prevention of Cruelty to Animals (ASPCA).

www.petplace.com/ reptiles/top-10-unusual- pets/page1.aspx
Approved by vets, a great place to find out about exotic pets.

www.rspca.org.uk/ servlet/Satellite?page name=RSPCA/RSPCA Redirect&pg=petcare
Pet care – know your pet. Expert advice from the Royal Society for the Prevention of Cruelty to Animals (RSPCA).

Index